Building My Footprint for God

Kenn Edwards

Copyright © 2020 Kenn Edwards

ISBN: 978-0-578-78961-3

Cover Art and Interior Design by Amy Allen
www.amysdesigns.biz

Published in the United States of America.

All rights reserved. No part of this publication may be reproduced, stored in a retrieval system, or transmitted in any form or by any means — electronic, mechanical, photocopy, recording, or any other — except for brief quotations in printed reviews, without the prior permission of the publisher.

Unless otherwise stated, Scripture quotations are taken from the Holy Bible, New International Version®, NIV®. Copyright © 1973, 1978, 1984, 2011 by Biblica, Inc.™ Used by permission of Zondervan. All rights reserved worldwide. The "NIV" and "New International Version" are trademarks registered in the United States Patent and Trademark Office by Biblica, Inc.™

Dedication

To my wife, LuAnn K. Edwards who has stood by my side through thick and thin. A true prayer warrior in Christ.

No time to read?

Keep up with your group by listening to the audiobook!

One-in-five Americans now listen to audiobooks according to Pew Research.

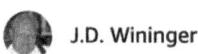 J.D. Wininger

★★★★★ **Forces You to Ask the Right Questions of Yourself...**
Reviewed in the United States on April 2, 2019

Download your copy today:

Table of Contents

Acknowledgments	9
Introduction	11
Week One ~ What's so Important About my Legacy?	13
Week Two ~ My Life is my Testimony	27
Week Three ~ Blessed Beyond Measure	41
Week Four ~ True Happiness	55
Week Five ~ A Good Steward Plans	69
Week Six ~ Ordinary People	83
Final Thoughts	97
About the Author	99
How to Host a My Footprint for God Legacy Weekend	100
Glossary of Terms	102
Forms	106
Endnotes	128

Dive Deeper with the audio podcast for each session.
Learn new insights from trusted advisors as
they bring their vast experience to life.
Listen as a group or one-on-one.

Visit **www.FootPrintForGod.com**
to download and discover more.

Special note to small group leaders. A resource to
assist you prepare for the discussion time is available online.
Look for the Facilitator's Help Guide in the downloads section at
www.FootPrintForGod.com/study-guide

This material has been prepared for informational purposes only, and is not intended to provide,
and should not be relied on for, tax, legal or accounting advice. You should consult your own tax,
legal and accounting advisors before engaging in any transaction.

Acknowledgments

Only teamwork brings a project like this together. Mentors, pastors, coaches, and many friends have contributed to my life and ministry over the past forty years. I am grateful for their labor of love.

I am thankful for the early critique readers who invested their time and experience to refine this study guide. J.D. Wininger, Mike Chapman, and Don Reed are true friends.

Plus, the brave souls who volunteered to be part of the first beta classes. Too many to name one-by-one but thank you to the Rio Rancho team for the first live class, and the pastors, authors (PJNET Family), and friends who made up the first Zoom class.

To God be the Glory for these true friends.

Introduction

We are at a crisis point in the United States of America, and it appears we could lose the race to evangelize our country. Left unchecked, Christians will face unparalleled persecution from society. Every believer should grasp the importance of teaching our children how to walk with God.

Building a godly heritage was on the mind of every Jewish father, even before his first child was born. During biblical times, the father would lay a foundation of their Jewish heritage as God's chosen people. So, each generation to come might know the Lord God Jehovah.

God's plan has always been for His children to have a heartfelt relationship with Him. Not a religious understanding because God said, "And these words which I command you today shall be in your heart" (Deut. 6:6, NKJV).

Teaching their family to fear (respect) God was a natural part of daily life. Every few weeks another feast or festival reminded the Jewish people of God's provision and blessing. Each feast retold the story of God's faithfulness. "…we will tell the next generation the praiseworthy deeds of the Lord, his power, and the wonders he has done…so the next generation would know them, even the children yet to be born, and they in turn would tell their children" (Psa. 78:3b & 6).

We shouldn't be any different. Sadly, we have allowed the culture today to influence our family more than the Word of God. Some parents take the position "They can make up their own mind." Yes, children should make their own choice, but many parents have failed to lay a godly foundation for them to observe. If we are not careful, we could experience Judges 2:10b in our world: "…another generation grew up who knew neither the Lord nor what he had done for Israel."

God has placed an awesome opportunity in our hands—to live a godly example before our children, even our adult children—so they, too, will follow the Lord.

Building a footprint for God requires a God-focused life. Just as the Jewish people repeated the stories over and over again, we should remind our children and grandchildren of God's faithfulness each day.

Our life's mission should be, "…as for me and my household, we will serve the Lord" (Josh. 24:15b).

Week One

What's So Important About My Legacy?

Life is hectic. When young, we struggle with finances, family responsibilities, and getting established in life. As we age, we begin having health issues and wonder about our retirement years. At points in our life it would be easy to say, "Stop the bus—I'm getting off." But we can't.

In our consumer-based world, it would be easy to believe our greatest investment is the purchase of our house or the 401k. But it's not. Our children and grandchildren are our top priority. Investing into their spiritual development will bring the greatest reward. "Children are a heritage from the Lord…" (Psa. 127:3a).

My children are a gift from God. As a parent, it is my responsibility to empower them so they can live in their full authority as a Child of God. As our secular society becomes less tolerant of traditional values and our Christian beliefs, we must stand strong and demonstrate to our family each day how to live for God.

Teach your children what genuine success means—it's more than money. Show them how to give of themselves so others will know Christ. As a parent, "I have no greater joy than to hear that my children are walking in the truth" (3 John 1:4).

The steps we take today shape our footprint for God—so make each footstep count.

Week one is based on chapters one and two of the book, *My Footprint for God.*

Day One
What Is Legacy?

Our true legacy is intangible. It is more about our value system than money. We focus on tangible items because we can see and feel them—houses, cars, and bank accounts. But the intangible may be worth far more to our family. Listen to the wisdom of Solomon. "The memory of the righteous is a blessing, but the name of the wicked will rot" (Prov. 10:7, ESV).

Our legacy is living. It is ongoing, even when we are not thinking about it. Each day we are building our legacy, and even after our death, our reputation, our legacy, lives on. One definition of legacy is "anything handed down from the past, as from an ancestor or predecessor."[i] Synonyms for legacy are heritage and tradition. So, our legacy is much more than money, it is our life, our personal history, and the values we live, teach, and pass on.

Compare the lives and legacy of Robert and June.

Robert is the owner of a construction company in Cincinnati, with a net worth of ten million dollars. He is an excellent businessman, who loves his family and is known for a generous heart. As a believer, he wants to be a good example and teach his family how to walk with God.

June is a single grandmother from Denver. Her husband died when the children were young, and she never remarried. At times she needed to work two jobs to make ends meet. Her children watched as she trusted God for their basic needs, such as rent, food, and protection. God has been faithful, and all three of her children are now serving the Lord in ministry.

Q & A

Who do you think has the stronger legacy? Robert or June (circle your answer)

What makes his or her legacy strongest? _____

_____

_____

_____

In your own words describe intangible:

_____

_____

_____

Which of these qualities do you want to be known for:
(circle your answers)

| Caring | Honest | Loyal | Hardworking |
| Provider | Generous | Godly | Friendly |

Are there other qualities not listed here that you would like to be known for:

_____

_____

_____

Personal Reflection*

_____

_____

_____

_____

*Each day space is provided for you to jot down your personal notes, action items or comments for review later.

Day Two
Our Spiritual Legacy

Our spiritual legacy starts with our decision to be a follower of Jesus Christ. Legacy is built upon our relationship with God and the influence we have with the people we meet. Billy Graham said, "The greatest legacy one can pass on to one's children and grandchildren is not money or other material things accumulated in one's life but rather a legacy of character and faith."[ii]

Through our spiritual legacy, we have the opportunity to influence our grandchildren and even the great grandchildren whom we may never meet. If we fail, we could lose our family's Christian heritage.

Even if you did not grow up in a Christian family, you can change the future course of your family. By faith, trust God to break any generational curses or historical sin patterns from the past. Begin praying today for your family to know Christ.

Think of your spiritual legacy as a baton you pass to the next generation. Your children will carry that baton long after you have finished your portion of the race. Pass on your beliefs and the values important to you.

To inspire our children to live for the Lord, let them see our example of living by faith. Share your walk with Christ from the past and be open about what God is doing in your life right now. Let your children see both the good times and difficult times in your life.

Q & A

What values do you want to pass on to your grandchildren? _____
_____
_____
_____
_____

Who passed the spiritual baton to you? _____
_____
_____
_____
_____

Billy Graham said, we should leave a legacy of character and faith. How would you describe a legacy like this? _____
_____
_____
_____
_____

Personal Reflection
_____
_____
_____
_____
_____

Day Three
More Than Money

For many people, it's all about the money. Since World War II, America has experienced a wealth boom, and consequently the American dream has become materialistic. Wealth should not be the most important aspect of our legacy. Solomon said, "A good name is to be chosen rather than great riches, and favor is better than silver or gold" (Prov. 22:1, ESV).

So, is having money wrong? Absolutely not! Money can be a blessing or a curse, depending on how we use it. Many families have been blessed and use their wealth to make our world a better place.

Vince Ragitti made it big in the entertainment business. Not as an entertainer, but in the business of building movie sets and backgrounds used in movie productions. By his mid-40s, Vinny's net worth was $18 million because of his hard work and business skills. At age of forty-seven, Vinny had a life-changing encounter with Jesus Christ. Vinny had a big heart before his encounter with Christ, but his generosity increased even more. He established a $10 million endowment fund at his alma mater to fund scholarships for students interested in movie-set productions.

Wealth can also be a curse rather than a blessing. Henry Ford said, "Money doesn't change men, it merely unmasks them. If a man is naturally selfish or arrogant or greedy, the money brings that out, that's all."[iii]

Unfortunately, the natural inclination for most people is to freely spend any newfound money or inheritance. Your hard-earned money could be wasted in a short period of time. Leave a piece of yourself instead. Your footprint on this earth will affect future generations for Christ.

Q & A

What do you think you would do with $10 million dollars? _____
_____
_____
_____
_____

Henry Ford said, "Money doesn't change men, it merely unmasks them." What do you think he meant by unmasking? _____
_____
_____
_____
_____

What does it mean to leave a piece of yourself? _____
_____
_____
_____
_____

Personal Reflection
_____
_____
_____
_____
_____
_____

Day Four
Living With Purpose

The idea of passing the spiritual baton to the next generation may be a new concept for many. For an effective handoff of our family's spiritual legacy, we need to live authentic, intentional lives. Intentional living requires a decision and is not just hoping or trying to do our best, but it is intentional.

The first step in planning your family's legacy is talking about the values your family received from past generations and comparing those to your current family. For first generation Christian families, look for help from your mature Christian friends to point you in the right direction. Then look forward to the next generation keeping your family's purpose alive in your family legacy. Some families develop a family purpose statement or a family mission statement describing their family's priorities.

Another great way to build your family's spiritual footprint is by working together on a ministry outreach (help the homeless in your community) or take a mission trip together.

Q & A

What values did you receive from your parents or grandparents? _____
_____
_____
_____
_____

Describe some specific and intentional ways that you might pass the spiritual baton to the next generation. _____
_____
_____
_____
_____

What ministry outreach or service opportunities has your family been involved in? What kinds of projects could your family get involved in? _____
_____
_____
_____
_____

Personal Reflection
_____
_____
_____
_____
_____

Day Five
Keeping It Alive

There are many ways to remind our family of their Christian heritage. Telling stories from the past is a great place to start.

Stories are a great tool to keep the family history embedded in the minds of our children. Everybody loves a story, especially the details of one that makes them laugh. Stories that we hear over and over again become a part of our lives too. Research suggests our brains become more active when we tell stories. Maybe that's why a good story captivates us.

Every family has some hilarious moments that bind a family together, like this story from Kenn's family.

> One summer when I was about seven years old, we were traveling in South Dakota. We stopped for a picnic lunch at a roadside park. As my mom scurried around getting our picnic lunch on the table, my sister and I sat to eat. Soon Dad joined us. When Mom completed her tasks, she sat on the picnic table bench right next to my dad. The only problem was, all four of us were on the same side of the picnic table. Within a matter of seconds, the off-balanced picnic table flipped over on top of us! We were all sitting on the ground with our lunch in our laps!

Memories like these will keep a family laughing together for many years to come.

Q & A

Share a funny story about your family. _____
_____
_____
_____
_____
_____
_____
_____

What steps have you taken to preserve old photos and special items you received along the way? _____
_____
_____
_____
_____

What ways could you suggest keeping your family's legacy alive? _____
_____
_____
_____
_____

Personal Reflection
_____
_____
_____
_____
_____
_____

Conclusion

Keeping your spiritual legacy alive starts with knowing Christ. There is nothing like a consistent walk with God to strengthen our reputation, our testimony, and our spiritual legacy. Lasting impact happens when Jesus Christ is Lord of our lives.

"And the things you have heard me say in the presence of many witnesses entrust to reliable people who will also be qualified to teach others" (2 Tim. 2:2).

Week Two

My Life Is My Testimony

In 1985 a new type of car hit the showroom floors in America—an Eastern Bloc Soviet style car made in Yugoslavia called a Yugo. While popular in Europe, the car flopped here in the United States. It became the butt of many jokes because of the low quality and ugly look.

When Americans flocked to this low-cost foreign car, they knew something was not right. A cheap imitation will never gain credibility.

Like the Yugo, our world has become highly skeptical of religion. Tired of people who call themselves Christians when there is no fruit. We may deserve some of this scrutiny, but we must ask, have we lost our credibility?

Building our footprint for God begins with integrity. The people around us know our reputation—our testimony. We should be dependable, do what we say we will do, and never live with a double standard.

Not that many years ago it was said, "A man's word was his bond." Have we reached a point in America that our church pews are filled with Yugos? The church in America must never lose its credibility.

Week two is based on chapters two and three of the book, *My Footprint for God.*

Day One
Passion

During a business trip a few years ago, I was in a hotel fitness room. As I walked on the treadmill, I watched a thirty-year-old man drenched in sweat and gasping for air. He was pushing himself as if there was a drill sergeant breathing down his neck, yelling at him to push harder and harder. What I observed was passion.

Passion in life is good. Especially if that passion points people to Christ. Passion comes from a strong, heartfelt desire to achieve. Many businessmen are driven by making money. Artists are driven to perform because of the fame. Athletes, like this man, are driven to win an athletic competition.

Those observations make me ask, "Am I passionate about God?" Does my passion drive me into a deeper relationship with Him? Am I willing to study my Bible even when I'm absolutely drenched in sweat and gasping for air? We have time, energy, and money for other passions.

Q & A

Describe what a passion for Christ might look like in your life? _____
_____
_____
_____
_____

If you were filled with this kind of passion would it change your witness for Christ? Yes or No (circle your answer)
Why or why not? _____
_____
_____
_____
_____

List several ways to develop a deeper passion for Christ that you would like to implement in your life?
1)_____
2)_____
3)_____

Personal Reflection

_____
_____
_____
_____
_____

Day Two
More Than Superficial

Our goal should be a deeper walk with God, as opposed to a superficial life. We miss so much when our walk with God is shallow. But here is the dichotomy. According to Pew Research, there are 2.18 billion[iv] Christians on earth—the highest at any time in history. At the same time, Barna Research says in the United States, of those identifying themselves as born again Christians, less than nine percent have a biblical worldview.[v]

If you are not familiar with the term, a biblical worldview is someone who believes what God said in His Word is true and the Bible is the foundation of life.

For more than a superficial walk with God, we need to believe the Word of God is truth and relevant to our life today. "All scripture is given by inspiration of God…" (2 Tim. 3:16, KVJ). Several translations use the words "God breathed." God breathed or inspired means the Bible is more than just another book. It is God speaking to us.

Having head knowledge alone about God is not a relationship with Him. Only a deep personal relationship with Christ will result in life change. That life change brings eternal impact from our footsteps in this life.

Q & A

On the scale below circle the number that describes your confidence level in the reliability of the Bible as the inspired and inerrant Word of God.

<u>Low confidence</u>   1   2   3   4   5   6   7   8   9   10   <u>Very confident</u>

What do you think 2 Timothy 3:16 means when it describes the Bible as God breathed? _____

_____

_____

_____

_____

Is it possible to tell when someone has a deep walk with God? Describe how you might be able to tell. _____

_____

_____

_____

_____

Personal Reflection

_____

_____

_____

_____

_____

Day Three
Kenn's Testimony

During the early years of my life, my mom and dad were involved in a mainline denominational church. A good church, but the gospel was not clearly presented. I considered myself a Christian because I was at church every Sunday. I was baptized as an infant and joined the church in my pre-teen years, but I did not have a personal relationship with Christ.

I knew about God in my head, but I had not surrendered my life to His control. I did not have a personal relationship with Christ—a spiritual life.

Around that same time, our church welcomed a new pastor who knew what a life with Christ was all about. His passion for Christ was contagious, and our family experienced a spiritual renewal. Over the next few years my Dad, Mom, and I served on several Lay Witness Mission teams in various cities, and I went on my first international mission trip to Columbia, South America. God radically changed our family as we opened our lives to Him.

Q & A

How is a personal relationship with Christ different from wearing a Christian label?

___

___

___

___

___

What does having a spiritual life mean to you? ___

___

___

___

___

In what ways can the leadership of a church help the spiritual climate of a church? In what ways can they hinder the spiritual climate of a church? ___

___

___

___

___

Personal Reflection

___

___

___

___

___

Day Four
Influencers

Who in your walk with God has been the influencer for you? The person who inspired you to go deeper with God. We all need a friend or a family member who is consistent in their walk with God regardless of their situation.

In the early days of my Christian life, I could see the influence of a former pastor. His example taught me to expect miracles when I prayed. Pastor Don (who may be in heaven by now) had complete confidence in God's power and the Word. When he prayed, he knew God would answer that prayer. Because of this, Pastor Don's legacy is still living through my life and ministry.

LifeWay published the article, "Who Is Your Spiritual Hero?" They had collected stories from students about the person whom they consider their spiritual influence. Alicia Claxton shared her story about her dad, David.

"His faith impacted every aspect of his life—as a husband, father, friend, and pastor. He went to be with the Lord when I was in college, but his influence in the years I had with him lingers on. My dad never met a stranger and could strike up a conversation with just about anyone. ...he told people about Jesus because he never got over the beautiful gift of grace."[vi]

Many could tell wonderful stories about those who have impacted our lives. Now it's our turn to do the same.

Q & A

Who has influenced your spiritual growth? _____
_____
_____
_____
_____

What did that person do that helped you? _____
_____
_____
_____
_____

Who do you think benefits more from being a mentor? (circle your answer)
1) The Mentor   2) The one being mentored   3) Both

Why? _____
_____
_____
_____
_____

Personal Reflection
_____
_____
_____
_____
_____
_____

Day Five
A Dynamic Life in Christ

If you have never experienced God in a dynamic way, don't worry. Today is a great day to get a fresh start with God.

Many of us can remember the early days in our adventure with God. We would do anything for the Lord because of our zeal. If someone invited us to go work with the homeless, we were excited to share what Christ had done.

We need to rekindle that fire for God because our spiritual legacy depends on a strong walk with God. Here are three principles that will apply for anyone who wants a dynamic life with Christ.

Talk with God: A relationship requires communication. Paul said, "pray without ceasing," so have an attitude of prayer all day long—as you walk, clean house, or mow the grass—talk with God. Develop the discipline of systematic prayer. Every day, at the same time, make it a habit to meet with God via prayer. Many people like to keep a journal so they can remember how God answered their prayers.

Study the Scripture: Although reading or listening to the Bible is very good, studying the Bible develops a deeper understanding. A Bible study is a great place to start, especially if you have an excellent teacher.

Prepare for each lesson in advance, even if you are not leading the group. You will be amazed how the Bible comes alive as a seamless book from Genesis to Revelation. Then plan to teach or help with part of the lesson. It may surprise you how much more you learn when you to teach the class. Over time, you will have a greater understanding and a much better appreciation for the Word of God.

Develop a personal ministry: Engage in a community-based ministry. When you fellowship with believers from various churches, you will have a better understanding of the Body of Christ. Every community has outreach programs to help the homeless, collect backpacks for school children, wrap Christmas Shoeboxes, or many other causes. Make these a personal ministry. Go on a mission trip if you want to turn your spiritual life upside down for the good. Follow the desire that God has given to you. Grow in God's grace and learn to affect those around you.

Q & A

Is talking with God and prayer the same? Yes or No (circle your answer)
Why or why not? _____
_____
_____

Give three examples of community outreach programs that you could be involved in locally?
1)_____
2)_____
3)_____

Share a time you had to search the Bible to answer a question someone had confronted you with? _____
_____
_____
_____

What did you learn? _____
_____
_____
_____

Personal Reflection
_____
_____
_____
_____
_____
_____

Conclusion

For the Christian community to regain its credibility, our reputation ought to be strong. Our testimony can become stale over time and damage our footprint for God. Stale Christianity is one of the greatest dangers in the church today. Satan wants us to be ineffective, and complacency is one of his biggest tricks. If we only receive and never give of ourselves, we can become ineffective in our spiritual life.

Week Three

Blessed Beyond Measure

We live in one of the greatest times in history. Yes, our world has problems—many problems, but God is at work. There is a great harvest of new Christians in many areas of the world, but not the United States, Europe, or Australia.

In the developed world, we have wealth and comfort well beyond my expectations. Technology continues to change our lives. We have great healthcare and our economy is growing. Life is good even with the ups and downs of life.

This has not always been the case. Life has changed drastically in my lifetime. Growing up we had a black and white television with only two local stations. Our home phone was a party line shared by multiple families. It might surprise you, but most rural farming communities did not have electricity until after World War II, just seventy-five years ago.

Have we learned to depend upon ourselves rather than God? Are we spoiled by our lifestyle?

It would be easy for us to look at all the negative in the world, but we are truly blessed. God continues to pour His blessings on America because of our faithfulness to send the gospel to the world.

Week three is based on chapters four and five of the book, *My Footprint for God*.

Day One
Surprise in Africa

I'll never forget the experience. The year was 1995—my first trip to Africa. I had always dreamed of traveling to Africa because I had heard how interesting the Ivory Coast and Cape Town, South Africa, were to visit. But I had never heard of Burkina Faso.

We landed late at night in Ouagadougou, so we drove to the hotel in the dark. The next morning, I rose early to get my first glimpse of the capital city of Burkina Faso. I had envisioned wild African safaris, the colorful clothing of the African warriors and the exotic foods.

I pulled back what appeared to be an old bedspread hung across the window. I was surprised to see dirt streets for roads in the capital city. Across the street from my hotel was a street market in full swing selling goats, chickens, fruit, and other foods I did not recognize. Everything was covered with flies and dirt. I was in shock.

Our driver came early to pick us up because we had to travel about 100 kilometers to the first village. Along the way I saw the grass huts that I had envisioned in the countryside. The mud huts had no electricity, no running water, and no inside toilets. Much to my amazement, I found people who were happy, even though they did not have all the things of life that I was accustomed to.

The lesson I learned is that money doesn't bring happiness. In the villages of Haiti, the slums in India, the dirt streets of Burkina Faso, people are poor, yet they have happiness. In America, from the plains of the Midwest to the shores of the Pacific, or on the busy streets of a major city, people are rich compared to the rest of the world, yet we can't find happiness.

Q & A

Describe how you would have felt riding through the villages of Burkina Faso.

_____
_____
_____
_____

Does it surprise you the people had contentment? Yes or No (circle your answer)
Why or why not? _____

_____
_____
_____
_____

What lessons can we take away from this story? _____

_____
_____
_____
_____

Personal Reflection

_____
_____
_____
_____
_____

Day Two
He Did What?

Stanley Tam grew up in Lima, Ohio. In 1936, he started his first company called TAMCO, and it failed miserably. He was going to give up, when he felt the Lord encouraging him to press on.[vii] With only $25 to his name, he started again with God as his partner. Slowly U.S. Plastic Corporation made a profit.

In 1955, while watching people at the altar at the front of his church, God asked Mr. Tam, "If a soul is the greatest value in all the world, then what investment can you make that will pay you the greatest dividends a hundred years from now?"[viii]

Stanley Tam was already giving 60-percent of the income from U.S. Plastic Corporation to God's work, but on January 15, 1955, he told God that he would give the entire business to Him.

They said it could not be done, but Stanley Tam made God the owner of his business.

To date, the businesses Stanley Tam built (which are wholly owned by a non-profit organization) has generated more than $140 million toward the work of the Lord. Mr. Tam's business legacy (and spiritual legacy) will pay dividends many years after his death—reaching thousands of people every year with the Good News of Jesus Christ. Stanley Tam understood that everything belonged to God and that changed the way he lived.

The story of Stanley Tam is counterculture for most Americans, but this idea is biblical. God is not asking us to give everything but be willing to obey Him.

Q & A

Do you agree with Mr. Tam that everything belongs to God?

Yes or No (circle your answer)

Take a moment to reflect on how you answered the previous question. What are the implications of this answer in your life? _____

_____

_____

_____

_____

In what ways is this concept countercultural? _____

_____

_____

_____

_____

Personal Reflection

_____

_____

_____

_____

_____

_____

Day Three
Recognizing It's Not Mine

If we took a survey next Sunday at your church asking, "Do you know that God owns everything?" A high percentage of your fellow Christians would say, "Yes, God owns it all." This concept has been an accepted teaching in the church for years.

Yet many of those same churchgoers who believe God owns it all, spend money as if it were their own. We make financial decisions every day, and we rarely consult God about the way we spend our money. Our rationale is: I worked hard to earn everything I have—my car, my house, and my bank account. It was my blood, sweat, and tears so I can do what I want with it.

We know God owns it all, but somehow a disconnect happens between our head and our heart. Intellectually we believe God owns it all, but for some reason knowing this fact has not changed the way we live. This concept has never truly penetrated our heart.

It might surprise you, but the Greek words in the New Testament for stewardship are translated as manager, steward, or administrator. These words reflect our role as a steward and not the owner. "The earth is the LORD's and the fullness thereof, the world and those who dwell therein…" (Psa. 24:1, KJV). Ultimately everything we have is from God. We may have purchased it with the money from our bank account, but it is God who gave us the ability to earn a living and accumulate savings. Stewardship is managing the property that God has entrusted to us.

Stewardship and discipleship go hand-in-hand. When we deepen our relationship with God to the point that we give Him control of the way we handle our finances, we walk in Biblical Stewardship.

Q & A

How large does a financial decision have to be before you talk to God about that decision? (circle your answer)

1) Less than $500   2) $500-1,000

3) over $1,000   4) Don't know

Do you think more people are likely to believe God owns everything with their head than with their heart? Yes or No (circle your answer)
Why or why not? _____
_____
_____
_____
_____

Describe how stewardship and discipleship go together.
_____
_____
_____
_____
_____

Personal Reflection
_____
_____
_____
_____
_____

Day Four
God's Manager

It is important to remember that all our material possessions are really blessings from God. His plan is for us to use money wisely, multiply it, and use all of it for His glory. We find the best example of this concept in Scripture in the parable of the talents. (See Matthew 25.) In this parable, a master called three of his servants in and put into their care a sum of money/property.

"For it will be like a man going on a journey, who called his servants and entrusted to them his property. To one he gave five talents, to another two, to another one, to each according to his ability. Then he went away" (Matt. 25:14-15, ESV).

The master gave each servant the talents expecting him to put it to good use and care for the master's money just as he (the master) would have. When the master returned, he was expecting to get more than he had given to each servant.

In a similar way, if my uncle puts me in charge of his business for two months while he is out of town, I would be obligated to manage the business for him in the same way he would handle it. In reality, I would be more careful with each decision because it was not my money.

True stewardship teaches us we should do the same with the possessions God has put into our care.

Scripture says when the master came back, he asked each servant to give an account of what they had done with the money. The master said to the servants who doubled the talents, "Well done, good and faithful servant." Then the master called the servant who buried the one talent, a slothful servant, "…you ought to have invested my money with the bankers, and at my coming I should have received what was my own with interest" (Matt. 25:27, ESV).

While there are several truths to learn from this parable, the key point is the master trusted the servants with his money and expected them to manage it wisely. In the same way God expects us to manage His money wisely. If we understood this concept, we might handle the money and property God has given us in a much different way.

Q & A

Why do you think the master gave different amounts of money to each servant?

_____
_____
_____
_____

How would you handle money differently if it belonged to your boss and not you?

_____
_____
_____
_____

Since God is the owner and we are the manager of everything we call our own, shouldn't we manage God's money differently? Yes or No (circle your answer) Why or why not? _____

_____
_____
_____
_____

Personal Reflection

_____
_____
_____
_____
_____

Day Five
Blessed to Be a Blessing

So why are we blessed? We may not realize this, but most Americans are in the wealthiest 3-percent of the world.[ix] That is hard for us to comprehend. We have become so accustomed to our lifestyle that we have lost touch with the rest of the world. Stop and think—50-percent of the world lives on $2 a day or less.

We can quickly see that we are rich in many ways. Jesus said, "It is easier for a camel to go through the eye of a needle than for a rich person to enter the kingdom of God" (Matt. 19:24, KJV). When the Scripture talks about the rich of the world—it is talking about us. The truth is, we are blessed to be a blessing.

Our happiness does not come from acquiring more, it comes through living our lives with purpose. The reason some of us always want more and more is to fill the emptiness is in our hearts.

When we miss God's purpose for our lives, we feel incomplete. But when we find our purpose and allow God to direct our steps, it will change others for eternity. That's how we find completeness and fulfillment.

God has blessed you and me financially for three reasons. First, to meet our needs—not everything that we want, but everything necessary to care for our families. Second, God wants us to put our finances to work and multiply it, as in the parable of the talents. Third, to release more resources into His Kingdom work.

Q & A

Do you agree with the statement that Americans are among the richest of the world? Yes or No (circle your answer)

Describe how it makes you feel that 50-percent of the world lives on $14 or less each week? _____

_____

_____

_____

_____

Does acquiring more equate to happiness? Yes or No (circle your answer)
Why or why not? _____

_____

_____

_____

_____

Personal Reflection
_____

_____

_____

_____

_____

_____

Conclusion

Look at everything God has put into your hands. You are truly blessed. We are blessed for a reason; to take the Gospel to the ends of the earth. Don't take those blessings for granted. God has a plan to use you to change our world.

Week Four

True Happiness

It's not what you think. The modern theory of happiness is more stuff equals happiness. But is that true?

Several years ago, our pastor gave a sermon series entitled "Stuff." He asked the men to count the shirts in their closet. To be fair, he also gave a similar assignment to the ladies to count their shoes.

Between the dress shirts, casual shirts, work shirts, long sleeve, short sleeve, sweatshirts, etc., I had over 100 shirts in my closet. I was not alone.

Pastor's message: we love our stuff, but it will never bring lasting contentment in life.

Week four is based on chapters four, five, and six of the book, *My Footprint for God*.

Day One
Stewardship Is a Lifestyle

So why should I include God in the financial decisions of my life? First, it is God who gives you the strength, knowledge, and ability to earn a living. "You shall remember the Lord your God, for it is he who gives you power to get wealth..." (Deut. 8:18, ESV).

We may take this for granted, but God is the one who gave us our health, mental capacity, and stamina to work every day. He also gives us the intellect to save money and the desire to accumulate the possessions we call our own wealth.

The second part of God's covenant with man in Deuteronomy 8:18 is to bless us so He (God) can reveal His glory in the world. Look at the latter part of verse 18, "...he who gives you power to get wealth, that he may confirm his covenant that he swore to your fathers…" (Deut. 8:18, ESV).

When God's children walk in His blessings, it reveals the power of God to the world. But when strapped with debt, and live paycheck to paycheck, we lose the ability to go, do, and give to support God's Kingdom work. What happened in the past is history. You can't change the past, but we can take steps today to improve our situation so God's blessings can flow through us.

As Christ's Ambassadors (2 Cor. 5:20) we are His representatives to the world. When we honor God in our lifestyle, we proclaim His glory. Unfortunately, many Christians handle their finances no differently from the rest of the world.

As God's steward the goal should be to have the highest credit scores, the lowest late payment rates, and rarely, if ever, should we file for bankruptcy. God's plan is that every part of our life including our finances point people to Christ. When our finances are out of balance with God's plan, the Kingdom of God suffers.

Q & A

Like all Americans you probably have made mistakes in the way you handled your finances. But would you agree that our goal as Christians should be to live within our means, pay our bills on time and walk in financial integrity? Yes or No (circle your answer)

Why or why not? _____
_____
_____
_____

Describe in your own words what it means to give God control of your finances?
_____
_____
_____
_____

In what ways could God's Kingdom suffer when a Christians' finances are out of balance? _____
_____
_____
_____

Personal Reflection
_____
_____
_____
_____
_____
_____

Day Two
God's Plan—
Everything for His Glory

When we see God's plan for our lives, we will recognize we are stewards and God is the owner. Clinging too tightly to our earthly possessions takes the focus off God and puts it back on us. Like in the parable of the talents, our goal should be to hear the words, "Well done, good and faithful servant" (Matt. 25:21) from our Heavenly Father.

When my friend Dick Spencer made his first trip to India, he thought he was fulfilling his life-long dream of going to a Third World country to share the gospel. While on that trip, Dick met a young pastor who had the same passion to share with the lost.

With seven families in a community surrounded by Hindu temples, the two of them, with God's help, started Hope Evangelical Church. A few years later they started New Hope School. The church grew to more than 250 families with 350 children attending the school.

Dick and his wife Sue have invested heavily in this ministry knowing it is making a difference for eternity. When the day comes that Dick and Sue can no longer travel to India, their lasting investment will be felt for many years to come. Dick believes everything we have as Christians is to be used to bring glory to God.

Q & A

Describe what it means to cling tightly to our earthly possessions? _____
_____
_____
_____
_____

Do you agree with Dick's statement that everything a Christian has is to be used for God's glory? Yes or No (circle your answer)

Starting a mission in India would not be an easy task. How would you feel about the investment of your time and finances in a local ministry project or in an international mission project like this? _____
_____
_____
_____
_____

Personal Reflection
_____
_____
_____
_____
_____
_____

Day Three
Giving Deepens My Legacy

Giving is a blessing we can enjoy, but it does not happen naturally. For most people giving is not easy. The tithe or some type of proportional giving is an indicator of our obedience to God. "Honor the Lord with your wealth and with the firstfruits of all your produce…" (Prov. 3:9, ESV).

Giving by faith helps break the stronghold of our self-will. It forces us to depend on God. Giving takes us closer to a self-surrendered life. It's not that God needs our money. But giving confirms that we have given God control of both the material and spiritual parts of our lives.

Giving also deepens our legacy. Every dime we give to God's Kingdom work becomes our ministry too. When that orphan child we support goes into ministry, they become a part of our spiritual heritage building our footprint for God.

Walking in God's Circle of Blessings is a place we all should desire. God blesses you so you can be a blessing to others. When you sow into God's Kingdom, Christ is lifted up. You see the fruit of your giving and that draws you closer to God. He continues to pour out His blessings upon you, so you can continue to give and support God's Kingdom work. Keep this circle working in your life and receive many spiritual blessings for which money can't buy.

Q & A

On the scale below, rate yourself. How do you feel about the statement "giving is not easy for most people."

<u>Hard to give</u>   1   2   3   4   5   6   7   8   9   10   <u>Easy to give</u>

Share what number you chose and why you chose it.

_____
_____
_____
_____

Some type of proportional giving (a percentage of your income) is a sign of obedience to God. Do you agree? Yes or No (circle your answer)

Why or why not? _____
_____
_____
_____

How does giving break the stronghold of our self-will? _____
_____
_____
_____

Personal Reflection

_____
_____
_____
_____
_____
_____

Day Four
I Can't Afford to Give

With our lifestyle many Christians say, "I can't afford to give," but I say, "You cannot afford not to give."

Several years ago a friend told me about their adult children moving to a dangerous part of the world on the mission field. As I expressed concern, he surprised me when he said, "They are safer in a country like Sudan in the will of God, than living in the United States and out of God's will."

Giving is much the same way. You are safer honoring God with your first fruits than keeping the money. Walking with God, in His will, brings protection, security, and peace even in the midst of the storm. (See Malachi 3:11.)

Even if you are on the verge of filing bankruptcy, honor God by giving something. It is a matter of the heart. If money is too tight, bring value to your church by mowing the grass or cleaning the inside of the building.

We may hurt ourselves by not honoring God with our giving. According to the USA Today, churchgoers give an average of 2.58^x-percent of their income, and that includes those who give well over a 10-percent tithe.

The joy of giving requires risk in trusting God. He says in Malachi 3:10, "…Test me in this," I will meet your needs.

True freedom comes with a balanced lifestyle. "Whoever loves pleasure will be a poor man…" (Prov.21:17, ESV). When we control our spending, we can pay off debt, save for tomorrow and walk in God's abundant blessings.

Q & A

Why do you think some believers say they cannot afford NOT to give? _____
_____
_____
_____

Have you experienced a time when you have seen God's provision upon your life/family because of your faithfulness to give even during difficult times?
Yes or No (circle your answer)
Please share your experience _____
_____
_____
_____

Do you agree that someone who honors God with their finances, walks in His favor and protection? Yes or No (circle your answer)
What does it mean to honor God? _____
_____
_____
_____

Personal Reflection
_____
_____
_____
_____
_____
_____

Day Five
Generosity

Generosity comes from the heart and it affects every area of our life. The concept of generosity and unselfishness go hand-in-hand. Someone who is unselfish cares for the needs of others even over their own needs. Similarly, a generous person is happy to give time, money, or other necessities unselfishly for the benefit of someone else.

Giving generously is birthed out of a lifestyle that recognizes God owns everything, and we have been blessed to give. It is not measured merely by the amount we give, but the attitude in which we give. A generous giver does not look at giving as a burden but a pleasure because they have an eternal perspective. They see giving as an act of worship to our Lord, and their only motivation is to lift up Jesus Christ for all the world to see.

Several years ago, on one of my work trips I met Patty. She lived in a small rugged house in the backwoods of Colorado. As a widow, she only received a small pension from her late husband and her Social Security, yet she still gives about 30-percent of her income away. By American standards, she does not have very much. Her house needed a new roof and the carpeting had seen its better days.

During one of my visits, I asked her about fixing up her house, but she hated to spend the money on herself when there were so many needs in God's Kingdom work. Patty truly has a passion to give to God, and her footprint on this earth will point people to Christ for years.

Most of us do not know what it means to sacrifice. When was the last time you gave up a meal so someone in another country could have a meal of beans and rice?

Later I learned how God provided for Patty. During the height of an oil boom, several investors starting buying property all around Patty's house. She was reluctant to sell, but the price they offered was almost too good to be true. Patty took the cash and purchased a much newer home in town with new carpeting and a new roof.

Because of Patty's faithfulness to God in giving, God provided abundantly more than she ever expected.

Q & A

Describe why generosity should come from the heart? _____
_____
_____
_____
_____

Do you really believe God provided for Patty? Yes or No (circle your answer)
Why? or why not? _____
_____
_____
_____
_____

Why is being generous so difficult? _____
_____
_____
_____
_____

Personal Reflection
_____
_____
_____
_____
_____

Conclusion

All of us should live generously, but doing so requires faith. It all starts with the heart and whether you are willing to do whatever God asks. "For where your treasure is, there your heart will be also" (Matt. 6:21)

As we allow God to work through us, we will see lives transformed by His power. That builds our legacy.

Week Five

A Good Steward Plans

The cook follows a recipe, the coach builds a game plan, and the carpenter follows a set of blueprints. Our spiritual legacy has more to do with creating an estate plan than you might think. A holistic view of stewardship should include estate planning because a good plan is designed so we finish well.

When our son was seven years old, he wanted to do something special for his mother. She was not feeling well, and he wanted to cheer her up. His big idea was to prepare breakfast for her in bed.

He found the pancake recipe and followed it to the tee, except he added one quarter cup of baking soda instead of one quarter teaspoon.

Mom was very gracious, but his plan did not work. His intentions were spot on, but he lacked the experience to finish well.

Many of us don't know what we don't know. As with the wise carpenter who learned over time, measure twice and cut once. With planning, we should seek professional help so we will finish well.

As we begin the most technical portion of this study, do not allow the detail to paralyze you. Instead, use this information as a guide which motivates you to action.

Week five is based on chapter seven of the book, *My Footprint for God.*

Day One
Could This Happen to Me?

Rosie and Jose were married thirty-seven years when Jose unexpectedly died. Rosie was shocked by his death, but the events of the next few weeks devastated her.

Like most Americans, Jose died without a valid will. Because their house was titled in his name and Jose did not have a will, she lost control of everything and the state took control.

She hired a good attorney, but the state said she would only get 50-percent ownership of her house and the kids would get the rest. Rosie felt cheated because she had lived in the house for more than thirty years and wrote every single check for all 360 house payments.

Rosie would have been in a different situation with some basic estate planning. Unfortunately, in all fifty states, without an estate plan, your family loses control, and the government calls the shots. The tragedy is that 60-percent of Americans die without a valid will.

Leaving a properly designed estate plan gives a roadmap to those you leave behind. Think of your estate plan as the last example to your family, how to manage everything God has blessed you with. It's also a great way to share your faith in Christ and provide for the ministries you love. The simple steps you take today can shape your legacy and your spiritual footprint on this world for Christ.

Q & A

Describe how you would feel when the court took control of your spouse's estate, and made each decision for you after your spouse died? _____

_____
_____
_____
_____

Would you agree, by having your financial affairs in order, you are practicing good stewardship? Yes or No (circle your answer)
Why? or why not? _____

_____
_____
_____
_____

How would you feel if the state laws gave your children 50-percent ownership of your fully paid house after your spouse died? _____

_____
_____
_____
_____

Personal Reflection

_____
_____
_____
_____
_____
_____

Day Two
Unwanted Consequences

When someone dies without an adequate estate plan (will, trust, etc.), by law your state is required to make sure all their bills are paid, and their property is distributed to someone.

The technical term for dying without a will is dying intestate. In these cases, the state law dictates which relatives are to receive your property. Each state has their version of a will they use instead of yours, and your family has little to say in the process. Dying without a will makes your family scramble because nothing is planned. Many times, members of the family have no idea where to begin and feel shortchanged because the state is in control.

Sometimes this approach backfires and your property goes to unintended people. Take for instance the estranged father who collected one million dollars.

> "Kylie was twenty-two years of age when she died in a tragic accident. Kylie did not have a will and her estate received a $2M insurance payout due to her accidental death. Because she had not made a will, Kylie's estate was divided with 50-percent allocated to each of her parents. This was even though Kylie's father deserted the family when Kylie was six months old."[xi]

Stories like Kylie's and others are not uncommon: an ex-spouse who is still the beneficiary on a life insurance policy, an old 401k that goes to an old boyfriend even after marrying another, or the court says your child needs to go live with an aunt you dislike. All these situations could have been avoided with a basic estate plan.

Q & A

Do you think the estranged father should have collected the one million dollars?
Yes or No (circle your answer)
Why or why not _____
_____
_____

Why do you think people let circumstances keep them from getting a will? _____
_____
_____

Is estate planning (will, trust, etc.) part of providing for my household? (1 Tim 5:8)
Yes or No (circle your answer)
Why? or why not? _____
_____
_____

Do you like the fact that state laws will take control of someone's estate if they do not have a will? Yes or No (circle your answer)
Why or why not? _____
_____
_____

Personal Reflection
_____
_____
_____
_____
_____
_____

Day Three
Someday, but Not Today

Death is something we do not want to face. We know it will happen but believe that it will be years down the road, so why should I spend the time and money to establish a will today?

Here are some of the most common reasons people procrastinate.

I do not own property
It is too expensive
The thought is overwhelming
I'm too busy
Never thought about it
I'm too young
Too many decisions to make

Many people feel they do not have enough property to go through the estate planning process, but that is a false assumption. Owning property is only one of the reasons to have an estate plan.

Others say it is too expensive. This is a valid concern for many families, but there are options. Some have never heard good reasons why they need a will. We think it will never happen to us, so why make all those decisions today when I'll live another fifty years. We have no guarantee about tomorrow, so wisdom says be prepared today.

Where do you start? As a believer, start with your church. Your church office may have some resources to help get you started. Some larger churches may have access to trained people or staff members who can point you in the right direction.

Other organizations like the Christian Stewardship Network, Kingdom Advisors, or a number of Christian foundations may help you along the way.

Q & A

Why is getting started the hardest part about estate planning? _____
_____
_____
_____
_____

Many people feel it will be years before they need an estate plan. Is this a valid reason for not acting today? Yes or No (circle your answer)
Why or why not? _____
_____
_____
_____
_____

What are the best reasons for a thirty-year-old to prepare an estate plan? _____
_____
_____
_____
_____

Personal Reflection
_____
_____
_____
_____
_____

Day Four

Reasons You Need an Up-to-Date Will

It might be hard to understand how estate planning honors God. But as with any spiritual discipline in our Christian life, stewardship requires a willingness to follow God's plan. As the manager of God's property, each decision I make will affect my family for many years to come.

Consider these reasons:

1. Your family stays in control: Many people say we already have too much government interference. Having a will is one way your family can stay in control of your estate. All too often we fail to act on preparing an estate plan which puts our family under the authority of the state because we procrastinated.

2. You can name who you want to be your personal representative: Your personal representative (often called executor) has the authority after your death to act on your behalf to close out your estate. By picking someone you know and trust, your wishes are more likely to be carried out and the property distributed to those you want.

3. Name a guardian for your minor children: If you die without a will, a judge gets to decide who will raise your children. Your personal preference and your Christian values may not be considered by the court. Naming a guardian for your minor children in your estate planning documents will avoid this problem.

4. Avoids confusion at your death: It is difficult to lose a family member, especially when the death was unexpected. With an adequate estate plan, your family will have a roadmap of your final wishes.

5. It is good stewardship: As the manager of the property God entrusted to you, manage it wisely. Practicing good stewardship teaches us to manage our finances, debt, savings, credit score, and even our estate plan in a way that honors God. Doing so will teach our family to honor God in every area of their life too.

Q & A

Why do you think it is wise to name a guardian for your minor children? _____

_____
_____
_____
_____

By updating your estate plan today, you are more likely to uncover any potential pitfalls. Do you agree?

Yes or No (circle your answer)

Why or why not? _____

_____
_____
_____
_____

Why is it important to name a personal representative/executor you can trust? ___

_____
_____
_____
_____

Personal Reflection

_____
_____
_____
_____
_____
_____

Day Five
Estate Planning Basics

Several elements comprise a good estate plan. Your Last Will and Testament is the most basic estate planning document, but it does not apply to everything you own.

In addition, you should have a Living Will, Healthcare Directives, and a Power of Attorney for financial decisions. Estate planning laws vary from state to state, so they may use slightly different names in your area. See chapter seven in the book, *My Footprint for God,* for greater clarity. In the appendix you can find the Glossary of Terms, and a set of forms to help you organize your finances.

Your accounts that have a beneficiary designation and your home (depending on how it is titled) may bypass your will. Double check your 401-k and IRA accounts for the correct beneficiary as well.

Good intentions are not enough. Some time back, a friend was surprised to learn his father used a fill-in-the-blank Beneficiary Deed he found online. He completed the form transferring the house to his son at his death. His father even had a notary witness his signature.

Unfortunately, his father did not file the deed with the courthouse, so the Beneficiary Deed was not valid. His intentions were good, but he lacked the experience to finish well.

The key is being prepared in advance and not putting your loved ones through any additional trauma. Seek help from an advisor in your area. It may save you money in the long run.

This material has been prepared for informational purposes only, and is not intended to provide, and should not be relied on for, tax, legal or accounting advice. You should consult your own tax, legal and accounting advisors before engaging in any transaction.

Q & A

How can fill-in-the-blank forms become problematic? _____
_____
_____
_____
_____

In what ways can being prepared in advance be a good idea? _____
_____
_____
_____
_____

When was the last time you reviewed your beneficiaries? (circle your answer)

1) Less than 12 months   2) Over one year

3) over five years   4) Don't know

Personal Reflection
_____
_____
_____
_____
_____
_____
_____

Conclusion

Getting started is the hard part. Hopefully, you will find it is not as difficult as you expected. Identifying your assets and how everything is owned is a healthy experience. The worksheets in the appendix should help. You may find a beneficiary that needs to be changed or an old account that needs to be closed.

Don't put this off. It is important to remember that your estate plan allows you to direct how your estate is handled after your death. Not planning can jeopardize your legacy because you could lose control.

Week Six

Ordinary People

What has God put into your hands? How could He use it (or you) to impact our world? You will never know until you try.

The little Jewish boy only had five loaves and two fish, but Jesus created a miracle. Peter and John were known as unschooled ordinary men, but God used them in extraordinary ways.

What about a six-year-old? Could God use her? Katelyn was six when she learned about the need for clean water in the villages of Africa. This didn't seem fair. She had all the clean water she wanted. Doesn't everyone she asked?

She prayed for God to help her make a difference. "Katelyn started by saving her Tooth Fairy money, selling lemonade outside her house and planning a yard sale, where she sold lots of her clothes and toys."[xii]

In a matter of weeks, she raised $1,580 to help the boys and girls in Africa.

If God can use a six-year-old with great faith, how could He use you?

Week six is based on chapters eight and nine of the book, *My Footprint for God.*

Day One
Emma, the Retired Schoolteacher

Emma is a retired schoolteacher from Florida who never married. She never thought she could leave a financial legacy. She knew of rich people who had their name on a building because they gave millions of dollars toward a new dormitory, but she knew that was way out of her league.

She lived in a small one-bedroom condo and drove a ten-year-old Chevy. Having lived on one income all her life, she knew how to economize.

One of Emma's favorite pastimes was to walk on the beach. The ocean reminded her of the power and majesty of our God. She spent many evenings walking along the water's edge praying for her students, friends, and her church family. At times, the beach would be almost deserted, so her footprints were the only ones she could see.

Years before, as a young teacher, she set up a payroll deduction account designed for teachers. The agent who helped her open the account almost scolded her, "Never take money out of this account until you retire." Over the years she paid off her condo, and her payroll deduction account grew to more than $400,000.

When she met with her financial advisor, she named four of her favorite ministries to receive the balance in the account when she passed away. Through this one gift, Emma could have the greatest financial impact of her life. It thrilled her that she could leave a portion of her estate so others could hear about the Grace of God.

Emma's footprint for God will have a far-reaching impact upon God's Kingdom for years to come.

Q & A

Why do you think Emma saw herself as an ordinary person? _____
_____
_____
_____
_____

How would you feel knowing a portion of your life savings will go to God's work after your death? _____
_____
_____
_____
_____

Why do you think Emma's legacy gift could result in the greatest monetary impact of her life on God's Kingdom? _____
_____
_____
_____
_____

Personal Reflection
_____
_____
_____
_____
_____

Day Two
Desiree and Granny

Many Christians have considered giving a way of life. Desiree remembered her grandmother teaching her as a young child how to give. Each Saturday she walked next door to Granny's house to get her allowance—ten dimes. Desiree put one dime in a church-giving envelope and the other nine in her piggy bank. That weekly exercise embedded the concept of giving in Desiree's life.

Several years ago, when Granny went to Heaven, Desiree was reminded of Granny's faithfulness in giving. Even though her estate was small, Granny gave the family instructions to put one tenth in the church-giving envelope for Jesus. Granny's spiritual legacy will now live through Desiree and her children.

Like Desiree, many of you have been giving to the Lord's work all your life. Why not continue that tradition and give a portion of your remaining estate to God's work? It will teach your children about giving by your example. Plus, legacy giving is one of the easiest ways to give, and it keeps your options open in case of an emergency.

God wants us to plan for those unexpected medical expenses in life. Plus, with all the uncertainty in the world, we need to protect our savings. But once we pass from this life and are safe in the arms of our Savior, we will no longer need the 401-k, certificates of deposit (CDs), or the nest egg. As you plan for the distribution of your life savings, include your church and favorite ministries too.

Q & A

Why did Granny's influence have a great impact on Desiree's desire to give? _____
_____
_____
_____
_____

How do you think Desiree felt when Granny asked her family to make one final gift from her estate to support God's work? _____
_____
_____
_____
_____

List three ways to teach our children the importance of giving.
1) _____
2) _____
3) _____

Personal Reflection
_____
_____
_____
_____
_____
_____

Day Three
Billy the Saver

Billy's childhood memories were scarred when their family lost their home during the Great Depression. As a result, Billy had two goals in life—stay out of debt and save every penny possible.

One Saturday, Billy drove through a strange part of town. With the narrow streets and unkept buildings he thought, "I'm glad it's 9:00 in the morning." People were huddled up all over the place. It reminded him of the people who stood on street corners asking for help.

This stirred Billy to visit the local rescue mission. He could see the rescue mission was more prepared to help than he was, so he went to the bank, withdrew one of his CDs, and gave it to the rescue mission.

While Billy's gift came from money that he might never need, many seniors are reluctant to use those just-in-case-funds during their lifetime. This is normal. As you plan your estate, ask God how He could use you to spread the Gospel and build your footprint for God.

Q & A

In what ways do you think the rescue mission was better prepared to help meet the needs of the homeless than Billy was? _____
_____
_____
_____
_____

Did Billy make a wise investment? Yes or No (circle your answer)
Why or why not? _____
_____
_____
_____
_____

How would you describe just-in-case-funds? _____
_____
_____
_____
_____

Personal Reflection
_____
_____
_____
_____
_____
_____

Day Four
John Left His Heart in Mexico

It might surprise you, but almost everyone can have a financial legacy. You may not think of it as a large legacy, but there are many ways to leave a lasting impact from your life. The area that is often overlooked is giving through an estate plan. It is a great way to leave a lasting legacy for the Lord.

John Winters retired to Sun City, Arizona, after working for General Motors for thirty years. The major reason John moved to Arizona was the close proximity to Mexico and his mission project in Magdalena, Mexico.

It all started as a young man with his first trip to Mexico in 1975. John went with his pastor, and the mission bug bit him. He fell in love with the kids in the orphanage, but especially one of the little girls. Silvia stole his heart. John wanted to adopt her, but because of the legal requirements he was not able.

John continued to support Silvia while she grew up in the orphanage. Her life was changed because of the care she received with John's help. She had food, medical care, and the education she needed to thrive. The local church connected with the orphanage had a great influence in her life spiritually, and she found Christ as her Lord and Savior.

One Sunday, John's church had a special speaker. The guest preacher asked, "Does your work for God have to stop after your death?" John had never thought about his death in that way. He pondered the question and later spoke to his pastor.

His pastor told him with a good estate plan he could continue to send money to support the orphanage for many years to come. That news pleased John to know the orphanage in Mexico would live on because of his giving.

In the planning world there are many tools to accomplish John's desire for supporting the orphanage. The right tool is not the hard part. Finding those with a heart to transform the world is by far a greater challenge.

Q & A

How will John's legacy continue to grow by supporting the mission even after his death? _____
_____
_____
_____
_____

Why is it harder to find those with a heart to give than to find the right tool to accomplish this desire? _____
_____
_____
_____
_____

Share three ways the children like Silvia might benefit because of John's giving to the orphanage after his death?

1) _____
2) _____
3) _____

Personal Reflection

_____
_____
_____
_____
_____

Day Five
Ordinary People Like You

You may be like Emma, the retired schoolteacher, and think of yourself as an ordinary person. Being an ordinary person fits pretty much all of us, but God uses regular people to accomplish His will. With a quick read of Hebrews 11, we see many ordinary (regular) people listed as heroes of the faith.

Others who might be considered ordinary people were the three young Jewish boys, Shadrach, Meshach, and Abednego. When they refused to bow down to the idol. King Nebuchadnezzar had them thrown into the fiery furnace, but God spared them.

What about the obscure woman we only know as the Widow at Zarephath? With only a handful of flour and a little oil, God used her to provide for Elijah during a severe famine without depleting her supply of flour and oil.

These were regular people willing to let God use them to change their world. Have you ever dreamed how God could work through you? Your life and legacy could make an eternal difference for someone in this world.

Q & A

Why does God use ordinary people to change our world? _____
_____
_____
_____
_____

What does it mean to you that we are blessed to be a blessing? _____
_____
_____
_____
_____

What is one quality the Heroes of the Faith in Hebrews 11 have in common? ___
_____
_____
_____
_____

Personal Reflection
_____
_____
_____
_____
_____

Conclusion

Happiness does not come from acquiring more, it comes through living with purpose.

We are blessed to be a blessing. You may feel like an ordinary person, but God has blessed you for extraordinary reasons. Seek Him and find out how God wants to use you to change our world.

In your mind your legacy gift may only be the size of the five loaves and two small fish. But with God, nothing is impossible. Leaving a financial legacy is possible for each of us. Despite what you think, this may be the easiest gift you have ever given—and the reason why someone accepts Jesus Christ as their Savior.

Final Thoughts

When our focus is wrong it hinders our footprint. Building our footprint for God is more important now than ever. Now is the time for God's children to be intentional about their walk with Christ.

Take one look at our world and you can see the evidence that the end of time is near. Violence in the Middle East, threats of homegrown terror, the decline in social values along with apathy in the church makes us feel hopeless, but we are not without hope.

Putting the concepts of this study together and applying them in your life will make your footsteps more effective for Christ. The example of a Spirit-filled life will show your family how to live for God in what could be a difficult future. This realization alone should cause us to evaluate our walk with Christ and drive us to our knees.

Everything about my life should point others to the cross. My personality, character traits, the trustworthiness of my speech, my work ethic, and my reputation should line up with God's Word. I know I am not perfect. But I still should take control of my spiritual growth and not be a hindrance to the spread of the gospel.

Leading my family and reaching others for Christ is how I build my footprint for God. It is also how I will leave a lasting footprint in the sand that wind and water cannot wash away.

Be sure to check-out the podcast associated with the chapter, Final Thoughts at www.FootPrintForGod.com/study-guide.

About the Author

Kenn is a speaker, author, and financial coach. He helps Christians develop a biblical understanding of stewardship and answers the question, "Why has God blessed me?" His passion is helping people build their spiritual legacy and leave their footprint on this earth.

His background includes financial planning and estate planning, and he holds the designation as a Chartered Financial Consultant ChFC® and a Certified Kingdom Advisors CKA®.

Kenn has served on the headquarters staff of Faith Comes by Hearing and The Gideons International. He worked as a Financial Advisor with American Express Financial Advisors and as a Vice President in Wealth Management for First Tennessee Bank.

Kenn's diverse background helps him identify with people from all walks of life.

How to Host a My Footprint for God Legacy Weekend

The My Footprint for God Legacy Weekend is designed to motivate Christians with their spiritual legacy, develop a biblical understanding of stewardship, and discover that estate planning is part of good stewardship.

Legacy planning has been long overlooked in the church, and most Christians have failed to protect their family with an adequate estate plan. Many believers equate giving as stewardship. True biblical stewardship is much more than giving. Stewardship encompasses all areas of our life, including money and giving.

Facts:
In 2011, 86-percent of Southern Baptist Churches did not provide legacy training to their membership in the previous year.
60- to 70-percent of Americans die without a valid will, which gives the government complete control of the family's estate.

Description of possible events:

General Awareness—Sunday Worship Special Event
Designed to give an overview of biblical stewardship and our role as God's steward. Stresses the importance of building our legacy each day with a call to financial accountability and estate planning.

Senior Adults—Recognition Dinner to the Honor Senior Adults
Celebrate the life and legacy of our senior adults with the goal to help them finish strong. Stresses the need for legacy planning and estate planning as a part of biblical stewardship.

Young Families—Saturday Workshop
Build a foundation of biblical stewardship and why good money management is important. Young families will learn how to build a godly legacy and how financial planning and estate planning can protect the needs of the family.

Complex Planning—Special Luncheon
Each church has a small percentage of people with more complex planning needs. Business owners, individuals with complex trusts or those who have accumulated wealth.

My Footprint for God Legacy Weekend is a great way to launch a My Footprint for God small group in your church. This weekend is designed to increase the awareness of our Christian legacy within the church, plus teach God's ownership of all as part of biblical stewardship.

Note: The author does not provide any legal or financial services and does not sell any products.

To find out more or to schedule an event, contact Kenn Edwards at kenn@footprintforgod.com.

Glossary of Terms

Estate Planning: The act of preparing for the transfer of a person's wealth and assets after his or her death.

Last Will and Testament: A legal document that communicates a person's final wishes pertaining to assets and dependents.

Personal Representative: The legal representative sometimes called the executor for the estate of a deceased person.

Codicil: An addition or supplement that explains, modifies, or revokes a portion of your Last Will and Testament.

Probate: The court process by which a Will is proved valid or invalid. Probate involves collecting the decedent's assets, paying necessary taxes, and distributing property to heirs.

Intestate: Not having made a will before one dies.

Living Trust: An effective estate-planning tool for avoiding the costs and hassles of probate, preserving privacy, and preparing your estate for transition after you die.

Irrevocable Trust: A trust where its terms cannot be modified, amended, or terminated.

Minor Trust: Is designed to manage and protect assets for a child until they reach a specified age.

Special Needs Trust: A legal arrangement that allows a disabled person to receive income without reducing their eligibility for the public assistance and disability benefits.

Trustee: An individual given control or powers for administration of the trust for the purposes specified.

Pour-Over Will: A legal document that ensures an individual's remaining assets *will* automatically transfer to their trust upon their death.

Living Will: A document that lets people state their wishes for end-of-life medical care.

Health Care Directives: A legal document in which a person specifies what actions should be taken for their health if they are no longer able to make decisions for themselves.

Financial Power of Attorney: A legal document that grants a trusted agent the authority to act on behalf in financial matters.

Guardian: The person who looks after a disabled person or a child whose parents have died.

Conservatorship: When the court appoints someone to manage an incapacitated person or minor's financial and personal affairs.

HIPPA: Health Insurance Portability and Accountability Act, a US law designed to provide privacy standards to protect patients' medical records and other health information.

Beneficiary: A person named to receive something from a trust, will, or life insurance policy.

Pre-nuptial: An agreement made between two people before marrying that establishes rights to property and support in the event of divorce or death.

Separate Property: Any property the spouses acquired separately before the marriage.

TOD/POD: Transfer on Death/Payable on Death, a brokerage or bank account with a beneficiary.

Beneficiary Deed: A type of real property deed used to transfer property at the owner's death.

Tax Deferred Assets: IRA, 401(k), 403(b) are tax-deferred accounts. That means you did not pay income taxes when you contributed the money. Instead, you will pay those taxes when you withdraw the money.

The Forms found in the appendix include definitions to several types of the property ownership.

This material has been prepared for informational purposes only, and is not intended to provide, and should not be relied on for, tax, legal or accounting advice. You should consult your own tax, legal and accounting advisors before engaging in any transaction.

Forms

In the pages that follow, you will find templates for lists and schedules you can use to organize your financial information.

These forms will help you bring all the information together in one place. More importantly, the information you record in these forms will be invaluable to those you leave behind.

If you would like full-page sized copies of these forms, you can download a copy at www.FootPrintForGod.com/study-guide.

Family Record

Contact Information:

Name_____
Address_____
City, State Zip_____

Home Phone_____ Work Phone_____
Cell Phone_____ Cell Phone_____

Do you have a written will? Yes or No (circle answer)
Where is your copy located_____
When was it last updated_____

Do you have Health Care Directives and a Living Will?
Yes or No (circle answer)
Do you have a Powers of Attorney (POA) for financial decisions?
Yes or No (circle answer)

Place where user names and passwords are stored_____
_____

This family record will give you a central source to collect your family and financial data. This is a good exercise for everyone, including young families and senior adults.

Young Families: This is a great place to begin understanding your overall financial picture.

Senior Adults: This record will be an essential guide to your family or spouse in the event of a sickness or death.

Family Member Name_____

Relationship_____ Birthdate_____

Social Security Number_____

Contact Information_____

_____

Family Member Name_____

Relationship_____ Birthdate_____

Social Security Number_____

Contact Information_____

_____

Family Member Name_____

Relationship_____ Birthdate_____

Social Security Number_____

Contact Information_____

_____

Family Member Name_____

Relationship_____ Birthdate_____

Social Security Number_____

Contact Information_____

_____

Family Member Name_____

Relationship_____ Birthdate_____

Social Security Number_____

Contact Information_____

_____

Key People to Contact in Case of Sickness or Emergency

Name of Person _____

Relationship _____ Phone _____

Address _____

_____

Name of Person _____

Relationship _____ Phone _____

Address _____

_____

Name of Person _____

Relationship _____ Phone _____

Address _____

_____

Name of Person _____

Relationship _____ Phone _____

Address _____

_____

Name of Person _____

Relationship _____ Phone _____

Address _____

_____

Name of Organization
Address
Phone
Name of Member
Membership Number

Name of Organization
Address
Phone
Name of Member
Membership Number

Name of Organization
Address
Phone
Name of Member
Membership Number

Name of Organization
Address
Phone
Name of Member
Membership Number

Name of Organization
Address
Phone
Name of Member
Membership Number

Income Sources (Social Security, Pension)

Type _____

Company _____

Payment Date _____ Amount _____

Location of Contracts/Records _____

Additional Information _____

Type _____

Company _____

Payment Date _____ Amount _____

Location of Contracts/Records _____

Additional Information _____

Type _____

Company _____

Payment Date _____ Amount _____

Location of Contracts/Records _____

Additional Information _____

Type _____

Company _____

Payment Date _____ Amount _____

Location of Contracts/Records _____

Additional Information _____

Type _____

Company _____

Payment Date _____ Amount _____

Location of Contracts/Records _____

Additional Information _____

Schedule of Debt

Type _____

Company _____
Amount Owed _____ Payment Schedule _____
Location of Contracts/Records _____
Additional Information _____

Type _____

Company _____
Payment Date _____ Amount _____
Location of Contracts/Records _____
Additional Information _____

Type _____

Company _____
Payment Date _____ Amount _____
Location of Contracts/Records _____
Additional Information _____

Type _____

Company _____
Payment Date _____ Amount _____
Location of Contracts/Records _____
Additional Information _____

Type _____

Company _____
Payment Date _____ Amount _____
Location of Contracts/Records _____
Additional Information _____

Cash Flow Worksheet

Get a better picture of your current spending by using the space below. Some items like mortgage/rent are a fixed expense. Identify expenses you could reduce today and apply toward your debt or building your cash reserves.

Expense	Budgeted	Notes
Mortgage/Rent		
Electricity		
Gas/Heating/Oil		
Water/Sewer/Trash		
Property Tax		
Phone/Cell Phone		
Cable/TV		
Internet		
Furnishings/Appliances		
Lawn/Garden		
Home Supplies		
Maintenance		
Groceries		
Misc. Supplies		
Clothing		
Cleaning Services		
Dining/Eating Out		
Dry Cleaning		
Salon/Barber		
Vehicle Payments		
Gas/Fuel		
Bus/Taxi/Train Fare		
Repairs		
Sub-Total		

Expense	Budgeted	Notes
School Tuition		
School Lunch		
Childcare		
Doctor/Dentist		
Medicine/Drugs		
Health Club Dues		
Auto Insurance		
Health Insurance		
Home/Rental Insurance		
Life Insurance		
Gifts for Family/Friends		
Church Donations		
Ministry Donations		
Emergency Fund		
Transfer to Savings		
Retirement (401k, IRA)		
Investments		
College Savings		
Student Loan		
Credit Card #1		
Credit Card #2		
Credit Card #3		
Other		
Other		
Other		
Sub-Total		
Monthly Grand Total		

Professional Advisors

Attorney _____
Contact Information _____

Personal Representative (Self) _____
Contact Information _____

Personal Representative (Spouse) _____
Contact Information _____

Guardian of Children _____
Contact Information _____

Pastor _____
Contact Information _____

Primary Care Doctor _____
Contact Information _____

Other Doctor/Specialist _____
Contact Information _____

Other Doctor/Specialist _____
Contact Information _____

Other Doctor/Specialist _____
Contact Information _____

Other Doctor/Specialist _____
Contact Information _____

Dentist _____
Contact Information _____

Accountant or Tax Advisor _____
Contact Information _____

Investment Advisor _____
Contact Information _____

Banker or Trust Officer _____
Contact Information _____

Employer _____
Contact Information _____

Employer _____
Contact Information _____

Business Partner _____
Contact Information _____

Life Insurance Agent _____
Contact Information _____

Home Insurance Agent _____
Contact Information _____

Auto Insurance Agent _____
Contact Information _____

Child/Adult Care Provider _____
Contact Information _____

Neighbor or Close Friend _____
Contact Information _____

Neighbor or Close Friend _____
Contact Information _____

Neighbor or Close Friend _____
Contact Information _____

Parents _____
Contact Information _____

Parents _____
Contact Information _____

Parents _____
Contact Information _____

Children's School Contacts _____
Contact Information _____

Other _____
Contact Information _____

Other _____
Contact Information _____

Other _____
Contact Information _____

Other _____
Contact Information _____

Other _____

Types of Property Ownership

1. Sole Ownership occurs when a single person owns a complete interest in a property or asset.

2. Joint Tenancy is when two or more persons share equal interests in the property. Joint tenancy is not limited to spouses. Anyone can share joint interests with others.

3. Joint Tenancy with Rights of Survivorship (JTWROS) is another form of co-ownership with rights of survivorship.

4. Tenancy in Common own an undivided interest in property between two or more people. However, unlike other forms of joint ownership, these interests can be owned in different percentages.

Community Property States: Currently, 10 states have some variation of community property laws: Alaska, Arizona, California, Idaho, Louisiana, New Mexico, Nevada, Texas, Washington, and Wisconsin. In a community property state, any assets or income obtained during a marriage are not owned solely by either spouse. It is considered part of the "community" of the marriage, and thus each spouse owns an equal share.

Note: Each state may have slightly different options available. Please consult with a professional in your area.

Property Ownership Schedule

Home Owner(s)_____
Type of Ownership_____
Location/Description_____
Date Acquired_____ Location of Title_____
Additional Information_____

Rentals Owner(s)_____
Type of Ownership_____
Location/Description_____
Date Acquired_____ Location of Title_____
Additional Information_____

Business Owner(s)_____
Type of Ownership_____
Location/Description_____
Date Acquired_____ Location of Title_____
Additional Information_____

Timeshare Owner(s)_____
Type of Ownership_____
Location/Description_____
Date Acquired_____ Location of Title_____
Additional Information_____

Cemetery Owner(s)_____
Type of Ownership_____
Location/Description_____
Date Acquired_____ Location of Title_____
Additional Information_____

Other_____ Owner(s)_____
Type of Ownership_____
Location/Description_____
Date Acquired_____ Location of Title_____
Additional Information_____

Vehicle Ownership Schedule

Type_____ Owner(s)_____
Type of Ownership_____
Location/Description_____
Date Acquired_____ Location of Title_____
Additional Information_____

Type_____ Owner(s)_____
Type of Ownership_____
Location/Description_____
Date Acquired_____ Location of Title_____
Additional Information_____

Type_____ Owner(s)_____
Type of Ownership_____
Location/Description_____
Date Acquired_____ Location of Title_____
Additional Information_____

Type_____ Owner(s)_____
Type of Ownership_____
Location/Description_____
Date Acquired_____ Location of Title_____
Additional Information_____

Type_____ Owner(s)_____
Type of Ownership_____
Location/Description_____
Date Acquired_____ Location of Title_____
Additional Information_____

Banking & Savings Accounts

Checking Financial Institution/Company_____
Phone_____ Name/Owner_____
Location of Records_____ Account #_____
Beneficiary_____ Value_____
Dates (Purchase, Maturity, etc.)_____

Savings Financial Institution/Company_____
Phone_____ Name/Owner_____
Location of Records_____ Account #_____
Beneficiary_____ Value_____
Dates (Purchase, Maturity, etc.)_____

Type_____ Financial Institution/Company_____
Phone_____ Name/Owner_____
Location of Records_____ Account #_____
Beneficiary_____ Value_____
Dates (Purchase, Maturity, etc.)_____

Type_____ Financial Institution/Company_____
Phone_____ Name/Owner_____
Location of Records_____ Account #_____
Beneficiary_____ Value_____
Dates (Purchase, Maturity, etc.)_____

Type_____ Financial Institution/Company_____
Phone_____ Name/Owner_____
Location of Records_____ Account #_____
Beneficiary_____ Value_____
Dates (Purchase, Maturity, etc.)_____

Stocks & Bonds
IRAs Retirement Accounts

Individual Retirement Accounts, 401-k
Financial Institution/Company_____

Phone_____ Name/Owner_____

Location of Records_____ Account #_____

Beneficiary_____ Value_____

Dates (Purchase, Matures)_____

Individual Retirement Accounts, 401-k
Financial Institution/Company_____

Phone_____ Name/Owner_____

Location of Records_____ Account #_____

Beneficiary_____ Value_____

Dates (Purchase, Matures)_____

Retirement Plans, Pensions, etc.
Financial Institution/Company_____

Phone_____ Name/Owner_____

Location of Records_____ Account #_____

Beneficiary_____ Value_____

Dates (Purchase, Matures)_____

Retirement Plans, Pensions, etc.
Financial Institution/Company_____

Phone_____ Name/Owner_____

Location of Records_____ Account #_____

Beneficiary_____ Value_____

Dates (Purchase, Matures)_____

Annuities, Savings, Bonds

Financial Institution/Company_____

Phone_____ Name/Owner_____

Location of Records_____ Account #_____

Beneficiary_____ Value_____

Dates (Purchase, Matures)_____

Annuities, Savings, Bonds

Financial Institution/Company_____

Phone_____ Name/Owner_____

Location of Records_____ Account #_____

Beneficiary_____ Value_____

Dates (Purchase, Matures)_____

Stocks, Mutual Funds

Financial Institution/Company_____

Phone_____ Name/Owner_____

Location of Records_____ Account #_____

Beneficiary_____ Value_____

Dates (Purchase, Matures)_____

Stocks, Mutual Funds

Financial Institution/Company_____

Phone_____ Name/Owner_____

Location of Records_____ Account #_____

Beneficiary_____ Value_____

Dates (Purchase, Matures)_____

This material has been prepared for informational purposes only, and is not intended to provide, and should not be relied on for, tax, legal, or accounting advice. You should consult your own tax, legal, and accounting advisors before engaging in any transaction.

A Word About Beneficiaries

The importance of a beneficiary designation on insurance policies and retirement accounts cannot be overstated. In most cases anything with a named beneficiary bypasses your will or trust—it is not controlled by a will or trust.

Your beneficiary is the person who is entitled to receive the proceeds from the life insurance policy, retirement accounts (IRAs), or transfer on death accounts (POD). A beneficiary can be one or more individuals and even organizations such as your church or favorite ministry.

You should review your beneficiary information at least once a year to make sure everything is current. Certain life events such as a marriage, the birth of a child, or divorce should also trigger a review of your beneficiary information. This will save your family members unnecessary grief later on.

Typically, you can designate two types of beneficiaries:

1) Primary beneficiaries are first in line to receive the designated asset upon your death.

2) Secondary (or contingent) beneficiaries receive the asset if there are no surviving primary beneficiaries upon your death.

NOTE: Please make sure the bank, insurance company, or IRA custodian has the same beneficiaries listed on each account.

Life Insurance Policies

Type_____ Company_____

Policy#_____ Location of Policy_____

Primary Beneficiary_____

Contingent Beneficiary_____

Policy Owner_____

Person/Property Insured_____ Value(s)_____

Type_____ Company_____

Policy#_____ Location of Policy_____

Primary Beneficiary_____

Contingent Beneficiary_____

Policy Owner_____

Person/Property Insured_____ Value(s)_____

Type_____ Company_____

Policy#_____ Location of Policy_____

Primary Beneficiary_____

Contingent Beneficiary_____

Policy Owner_____

Person/Property Insured_____ Value(s)_____

Type_____ Company_____

Policy#_____ Location of Policy_____

Primary Beneficiary_____

Contingent Beneficiary_____

Policy Owner_____

Person/Property Insured_____ Value(s)_____

Other Insurance Policies

Home Company _____

Policy#_____ Location of Policy_____

Policy Owner_____

Person/Property Insured_____ Value(s)_____

Auto Company _____

Policy#_____ Location of Policy_____

Policy Owner_____

Person/Property Insured_____ Value(s)_____

Disability Company _____

Policy#_____ Location of Policy_____

Policy Owner_____

Person/Property Insured_____ Value(s)_____

Health Company _____

Policy#_____ Location of Policy_____

Policy Owner_____

Person/Property Insured_____ Value(s)_____

Other_____ Company_____

Policy#_____ Location of Policy_____

Policy Owner_____

Person/Property Insured_____ Value(s)_____

Other_____ Company_____

Policy#_____ Location of Policy_____

Policy Owner_____

Person/Property Insured_____ Value(s)_____

Cards (Credit, Debit, ATM)

Type_____ Name on Account_____
Account #_____
If Lost or Stolen, Notify Company/Institution_____
_____

Address_____
Phone_____

Type_____ Name on Account_____
Account #_____
If Lost or Stolen, Notify Company/Institution_____
_____

Address_____
Phone_____

Type_____ Name on Account_____
Account #_____
If Lost or Stolen, Notify Company/Institution_____
_____

Address_____
Phone_____

Type_____ Name on Account_____
Account #_____
If Lost or Stolen, Notify Company/Institution_____
_____

Address_____
Phone_____

Other Important Records

Adoption Papers Location _____
Additional Information _____

Baptismal Records Location _____
Additional Information _____

Birth Certificates Location _____
Additional Information _____

Citizen/Naturalization Papers Location _____
Additional Information _____

Death Certificates Location _____
Additional Information _____

Diplomas Location _____
Additional Information _____

Divorce/Separation Papers Location _____
Additional Information _____

Health Records (with Blood Type) Location _____
Additional Information _____

Marriage Certificates Location _____
Additional Information _____

Military Records Location _____
Additional Information _____

Passport Location _____
Additional Information _____

Real Estate Deed/Easements/Rights of Way Location _____
Additional Information _____

Titles and Bills of Sale Location _____
Additional Information

Titles and Bills of Sale Location_____
Additional Information_____

Bank/Credit Union Statements Location_____
Additional Information_____

Cemetery Plot/Records Location_____
Additional Information_____

Education Records Location_____
Additional Information_____

Employment Records Location_____
Additional Information_____

Family Medical History Location_____
Additional Information_____

Income/Expense Records Location_____
Additional Information_____

Income Tax Returns Location_____
Additional Information_____

Funeral Plan Documents/Instructions Location_____
Additional Information_____

Letter of Last Instructions Location_____
Additional Information_____

Medical Records Location_____
Additional Information_____

Net Worth Statements Location_____
Additional Information_____

Safe-Deposit Box Inventory Location_____
Additional Information_____

Warranties/Appliance Manuals Location_____
Additional Information_____

Endnotes

i https://www.dictionary.com/browse/legacy Sourced September 17, 2020

ii http://www.breakingchristiannews.com/articles/display_art.html?ID=9507 Sourced on March 20, 2015

iii http://www.breakingchristiannews.com/articles/display_art.html?ID=9507 Sourced on March 20, 2015

iv http://americamagazine.org/issue/5125/signs/pew-study-estimates-global-christians-218-billion Sourced on April 17, 2015

v http://www.christianheadlines.com/news/survey-only-half-of-pastors-have-biblical-worldview-1240810.html Sourced on April 26, 2015

vi http://www.lifeway.com/Article/Who-is-your-spiritual-hero-mentorship-march Sourced on March 30, 2015

vii http://www.giantsforgod.com/stanley-tam-us-plastic/ sourced March 14, 2016

viii God Owns My Business by Dr. R. Stanley Tam

ix http://www.globalrichlist.com Sourced on June 3, 2015

x http://usatoday30.usatoday.com/news/religion/2008-05-31-tithing-church_N.htm Sourced on August 7, 2015

xi http://www.pt.qld.gov.au/wills/stories.html sourced on August 30, 2015

xii https://explorer.compassion.com/thirst-saving-lives/ sourced December 19, 2019

www.ingramcontent.com/pod-product-compliance
Lightning Source LLC
Chambersburg PA
CBHW081458040426
42446CB00016B/3293